Backyard Animals
Butterflies

Jennifer Hurtig

Weigl Publishers Inc.

Published by Weigl Publishers Inc.
350 5th Avenue, Suite 3304, PMB 6G
New York, NY 10118-0069
Website: www.weigl.com

Library of Congress Cataloging-in-Publication Data

Hurtig, Jennifer.
  Butterflies / Jennifer Hurtig.
     p. cm. -- (Backyard animals)
  Includes index.
  ISBN 978-1-59036-683-7 (hard cover : alk. paper) -- ISBN 978-1-59036-684-4 (soft cover : alk. paper)
  1. Butterflies--Juvenile literature. I. Title.

QL544.2.H87 2008
595.78'9--dc22

                                                         2006102110

Printed in the United States of America
  2 3 4 5 6 7 8 9 0 11 10 09 08

Editor Heather C. Hudak
Design and Layout Terry Paulhus

Cover: Butterflies help many wild plants and important crops grow.

Contents

Meet the Butterfly

Butterflies are insects. Insects are small animals that have an **exoskeleton**. They do not have a backbone. The exoskeleton protects the butterfly's body.

Many types of butterflies have colorful wings. They use their wings to travel from plant to plant to sip **nectar**. Butterflies also use their wings to flee from **predators**. The fastest butterflies can fly at almost 30 miles (48 kilometers) per hour. The slowest butterflies fly at about 5 miles (8 km) per hour.

A butterfly begins life as an egg. It then turns into a caterpillar. To become a butterfly, a caterpillar spins a **chrysalis** around itself. The caterpillar stays in the chrysalis until it becomes a butterfly.

Fascinating Facts

Most caterpillars molt, or shed their skin, four or five times. This is because they grow quickly.

The clearwing butterfly has clear wings. This helps the butterfly blend in with its environment.

All about Butterflies

There are more than 18,500 known **species** of butterflies. They come in different colors and sizes. The largest butterfly is the Queen Alexandra birdwing, which lives in New Guinea. The smallest butterfly is the western pygmy blue. It lives in the United States.

Butterflies are similar to moths. However, butterflies are brighter in color. Moths are most active at night. Butterflies are busiest in the daytime. When butterflies rest, their wings stand up. Moths' wings lie flat when they are resting.

The female Queen Alexandra birdwing can have a wingspan of up to 12 inches (30.5 centimeters).

Where Butterflies Live

Blue Morpho Butterfly

- Lives in rain forests from Brazil to Venezuela

Julia Butterfly

- Found in South and Central America and the southern United States

Monarch Butterfly

- Found mostly in North America, and flies to Mexico each fall

Tiger Swallowtail Butterfly

- Found in the United States and Canada

Ulysses Butterfly

- Lives in Australia, Indonesia, and nearby islands

Butterfly History

Butterflies live in all parts of the world, except Antarctica. However, not much is known about where they first lived. This is because there are not many butterfly **fossils**. The oldest fossils are about 50 million years old.

Some scientists believe butterflies developed from an ancient type of moth. The moth may have lived 65 to to 135 million years ago. This is when the first flowering plants began to grow and dinosaurs roamed Earth.

At one time, people thought that butterflies flew into houses and stole milk. The word *butterfly* may come from the Old English word *buttorfleoge*. This means "butter fly."

Butterflies can be seen in old Egyptian paintings at Thebes. Thebes is an ancient city in Egypt. The paintings are 3,500 years old.

The brimstone butterfly has yellow wings. It is one of the first butterflies to be seen in spring. Some people believe butterflies may have been named for this butter-colored insect.

Butterfly Shelter

Butterflies live in open, sunny places. They live in fields of flowers, near the edge of wooded areas, along hillsides, and near streams. Butterflies that live in cold areas **hibernate** or **migrate** for the winter.

In the caterpillar stage, butterflies live on leaves, branches, or under sheltered surfaces. This helps them hide from predators. It also gives them a place to spin a chrysalis.

Caterpillars live near plants that they can eat. Caterpillars grow very quickly, so they must eat large amounts of food.

In winter, monarch butterflies fly south from Canada and the northern United States. They travel as far as 2,000 miles (3,200 km) to Mexico or California. Here, the weather is warmer.

Butterfly Features

Butterflies' bodies have many special features. They use different body parts to help them find food, eat, fly, and hide from predators.

HEAD
A butterfly's head has two **antennae**. Butterflies use their antennae for balance and to smell objects. Butterflies sip food through their proboscis. The proboscis is similar to a tongue. It is long and uncoils when the butterfly eats.

LEGS
Butterflies have six legs. Each leg has small claws at the end of them. Butterflies use their feet to taste food. The two front legs are sometimes shorter than the others. Butterflies use the front legs to clean their antennae.

WINGS

Butterflies have four wings. The wings are attached to the thorax. If their wings are torn, they cannot be fixed. As butterflies age, the colors of their wings fades.

EYES

Butterflies can see **ultraviolet rays**. Their eyes have many small lenses. These capture light from the butterfly's range of view.

THORAX

The thorax is the middle part of an insect's body. It is separated into three parts. There is a pair of legs on each part. The thorax has muscles that help make the wings and legs move.

What Do Butterflies Eat?

Butterflies eat the sugar found in tree sap and rotting fruit. They also feed on flower nectar and water from puddles.

Butterflies find their food by sight, smell, and taste. They use their proboscis to suck nectar or other food into their mouth. When they feed on flowers, they sometimes carry **pollen** to another flower. This helps plants to **reproduce**.

Butterflies like to eat from clusters of flowers that have wide, flat rims. This gives butterflies a large landing platform.

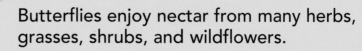

Butterflies enjoy nectar from many herbs, grasses, shrubs, and wildflowers.

Butterfly Life Cycle

Female butterflies lay many eggs on or near plants. They can lay eggs one at a time, in small clusters, or even hundreds at a time. The larval, or caterpillar, stage of a butterfly's life begins when the egg hatches.

Egg

The butterfly begins life as a small egg. The egg may be white, green, or yellow. Eggs are different shapes, such as oval, pod-shaped, or round. There is a yolk in each egg that will turn into a caterpillar.

Larva

The larval stage lasts from two weeks to one month. The caterpillar eats leaves and grows quickly. When the caterpillar stops growing, it stops eating. It then attaches itself to an object that will provide cover. This may be a leaf or a twig. The caterpillar then enters the pupal stage.

The pupal stage happens when the caterpillar is in a chrysalis. During this stage, a caterpillar becomes a butterfly. When the butterfly comes out of the chrysalis, it is in its adult form.

Pupa

The pupal stage can last from a few days to many months. The pupa does not eat. It hangs inside the chrysalis. The chrysalis often becomes clear the day before the butterfly comes out.

Adult

After coming out of its chrysalis, the butterfly has wrinkled wings. It uses fluid from inside its body to help plump up its wings. Butterflies then begin to search for mates. After they mate, the female lays eggs. The stages begin again. Some butterflies live for a few days. Others can live as long as 12 months.

Encountering Butterflies

Some people like to have butterflies in their garden. Butterflies will live in gardens that have nectar-rich flowers. Milkweeds, sunflowers, and chives will attract butterflies. It is important to plant a variety of flowers that bloom throughout the season.

Caterpillars can only eat certain types of plants. These are called host plants. Butterflies only lay their eggs on host plants. Willow is a common host plant.

Insecticides are chemicals that kill insects. They are harmful to caterpillars and butterflies. To keep butterflies safe, do not use insecticides in the garden.

Useful Websites

To learn more about creating a backyard home for butterflies, go to
http://butterflywebsite.com/butterfly gardening.cfm

Some people catch butterflies using nets. They must be careful not to harm the butterflies or their habitats. It is important to release the butterflies back into nature.

Myths and Legends

People around the world have different stories and beliefs about butterflies. Some cultures believe that they can predict the weather by watching how butterflies behave. In the Middle Ages, people thought that seeing large groups of butterflies meant that a war was about to begin.

Many ancient peoples believed that butterflies were symbols of human souls. The ancient Greeks and the Aztecs of Mexico believed that the spirits of people who had died took the form of butterflies. This allowed them to visit their living relatives.

In Greek, the word for butterfly is *psyche*. It means "soul" and "butterfly."

The First Butterflies

This Ojibwa Indian story tells how butterflies were first created.

A long time ago, animals helped Spirit Woman take care of her twin babies. The dog watched over the children. The bear's fur kept them warm. The deer gave them milk. The wolf hunted food for them. The birds sang to the twins. The beaver and muskrat gave them baths.

After a while, the animals noticed that the twins did not walk or run. The animals met with Nanabush, an Ojibwa spirit. Nanabush said that the children did not walk or run because the animals gave them everything they needed. Nanabush decided to find a way to make the twins walk.

Nanabush found sparkling blue, green, yellow, and red stones. He threw a handful into the air. He looked up and saw that the stones had turned into animals with brightly colored wings. These were the first butterflies. They followed Nanabush back to the children. The children waved their arms. Soon, they began walking to try to catch the butterflies.

Frequently Asked Questions

How can I tell if a butterfly is male or female?

Answer: Most female butterflies are larger than males. Males and females sometimes have different markings on their wings. Females are often less colorful than males.

Do butterflies and caterpillars have predators?

Answer: Butterflies have quite a few predators. Birds like to eat caterpillars. Spiders and other bugs eat butterflies. Some insects may eat a butterfly's eggs.

How do caterpillars and butterflies protect themselves from predators?

Answer: Some caterpillars are poisonous to other animals because of the food they eat. Other caterpillars have coloring that helps them blend into their surroundings. They may have spots on them that look like eyes. This makes them appear more dangerous. Butterflies can fly away from their predators.

Puzzler

See if you can answer these questions about butterflies.

1. How many stages of life does a butterfly pass through?
2. How do butterflies eat?
3. How are antennae used?
4. How many legs does a butterfly have?
5. In which stage does the butterfly not eat?

Answers: 1. four 2. They suck liquid through their proboscis. 3. for balance and to smell objects 4. six 5. pupal stage

Find Out More

There are many more interesting facts to learn about butterflies. Look for these books at your library so you can learn more.

Baran, Myriam, and Gilles Martin. *Butterflies of the World*. Harry N. Abrams, Inc., 2006.

Burris, Judy, and Wayne Richards. *The Life Cycles of Butterflies*. Storey Publishing, 2006.

Words to Know

antennae: long, thin body parts that extend from an insect's head

chrysalis: the hard covering that a caterpillar spins around itself

exoskeleton: a shell or protective covering

fossils: the hardened remains of animals or plants that lived long ago

hibernate: to spend the winter in a sleep-like state

migrate: to travel from one country or place to another

nectar: liquid food from plants

pollen: a yellow powder produced by flowers

predators: animals that hunt other animals for food

reproduce: to have babies

species: groups of animals or plants that have many features in common

ultraviolet rays: rays of light that are invisible to the human eye

Index